Developing Visionary Leadership

Richard Williams

Chief Executive of Options

Director of Consultancy for Paradigm

Mark Tanner

Vicar of St Mary's Wheatley, Doncaster

GROVE BOOKS LIMITED
RIDLEY HALL RD CAMBRIDGE CB3 9HU

Contents

The Cover Illustration is by Peter Ashton

First Impression July 2004
ISSN 1470-8531
ISBN 1 85174 567 X

Introduction **1**

Fantastic Leaders—God's Change Makers

We believe your church has the potential to lead the development and transformation of your local community into a passionate and purposeful place welcoming many people into faith. We believe that you and your team can develop and nurture dynamic, loving and serving disciples, in whom God is glorified abundantly every day of every week in all that they say and do.

Sadly the reality does not always match the aspiration. Nationally, local churches have taken a battering over the last few years. Numbers have fallen and we are accused of being irrelevant, boring, exclusive social clubs and much besides…and sadly some of this is true. Young people see with frightening clarity a credibility gap between our espoused values and what we actually do. The church of Acts excites us by its vibrancy, purposefulness and abundant love, and yet our own seems a pale shadow of what came first. Our touch does not match our words.

There are hosts of reasons why we have struggled, but one of the most important is that we have not recruited, trained, developed or nurtured spiritual *leaders*. Our model has been one of recruiting and training 'pastors' and relying on the old maxim that people will follow an educated man. This is not working. We live in a rapidly changing and increasingly secular world, where we need to meet people's needs in all sorts of different ways. Fantastic organizations, be they churches, charities, businesses or sports teams, have fantastic leaders. With great leadership our churches can be transformed into places where people are excited to belong, where faith is constantly growing and pouring out to share Christ in word and deed…and this change can only be driven and held together by prophetic, wise and courageous leadership, in the service of Christ.

If you are a church leader then the future is in your hands

What we are saying is that if you are a church leader then the future is in your hands. We believe that God wants to build an army of great leaders, men and women who will listen and respond to the Spirit's guidance, who are skilled in leading others and making change happen, who can empower and motivate others, who can work through difficult or complex situations and inspire others to do the same.

If that is you, or who you aspire to be, then this booklet is for you. It is a practical introduction to great leadership. We will suggest some key aspects of leadership, discuss how to get started, and give some hot tips for success. It is not a theorist's book. It has been put together by a chief executive of a large secular agency and a vicar of a very ordinary local church, arising from questions raised when walking their dogs, and is for those who want to get on and change things. In it we examine good secular models of leadership from a biblical perspective and we make no apology for this, frustrating though it is not to have more space to expand biblical models. Our aim is to grow the local church—because Jesus established it, we are proud to be part of it, the Spirit is working in it, and…*'Why should the devil have all the good leaders?'*

Manager or Leader—Which Are You Called To Be?

- **Leaders** are people who lead, enable and inspire—people who set direction. They decide upon priorities for an organization, and then enable them to be achieved.
- **Managers** are people who manage—people who efficiently follow an established path.

Have you analysed your time to discover how much of it you spend managing and how much leading? Most churches are 'led' by managers, by godly preachers, teachers or pastors who are not enabled to use those essential gifts in a leadership capacity. In a world of strong churches and little change this would be fine, but that is not our world—or our church. When you consider the struggles and challenges that most churches are facing and the rapidly changing fabric of society, it is not rocket science to work out that we desperately need leaders who will grasp the changes needed for the future and set clear courses to achieve them. We need leaders who will put aside the things that are not working, even the accepted, orthodox, or 'only' way of doing things, and find the new, fresh, innovative ways forward. A leader seeks the approach that strategically cuts to where change is needed and is bold enough to do it.

This is not a question of the faithfulness or 'validity' of our ministry. It is a question of how prophetic we are willing to be with our gifting—for the prophet will see beyond what is, to what God wills to be. The prophet will speak not what is easy but what is right. The prophet leads in the power of the Spirit. We need to be careful about terminology. In the Ephesians 4 sense I am a teacher and evangelist, that is my gifting, but I face a choice about how I use that gift. I can look down or I can look up. I can merely equip those around me to carry on in their discipleship or I can seek the Lord to inspire change. I can pastor from the pulpit or I can teach prophetically. I can be a manager or a leader—and the same is true for you.

This is a huge challenge, and yet with God's blessing, in his power, leaders can make an unimaginable contribution to the kingdom. Leadership is required in all areas of a church; whether it is worship, youth work, catering or finances. All require people who will act decisively to determine what needs to be done or set aside, and then inspire others to follow God's vision.

This role of leadership leaves the church with many questions. We call our leaders 'pastors' or 'priests' despite the confusion about what these terms mean or imply about our nature and priorities. Too often we train teachers, pastors, liturgists, and sandal-wearers, and then we place them in some of the most challenging leadership roles around. Should we be recruiting teachers, pastors or evangelists and making them leaders, or recruiting leaders (some who will probably have the gift of teaching, pastoring or evangelism) who then need to ensure the church is well taught, nurtured and that evangelism occurs?(We might debate which comes first, but the point is that we cannot do without either.) Joshua was appointed *primarily to lead* God's people and his mentor Moses had Aaron around to be his preacher and priest.

This question affects us at a local level as we shape the leadership teams in our churches. Leadership is the crucial dynamic in such a team, and it may or may not come from you. It is more important to do the right things than to do things right, to be effective rather than efficient, to allow space for the Spirit to transform and shape a dynamic community than preserve a building or club. Leadership is crucial for the church and if you are reading this book then it is likely that you feel called to some kind of leadership. How do you develop that gift? At heart you practise. We are going to spell out four vital elements of leadership in this booklet: vision; building teams; growth; and courageous activity. If you are a leader then read and lead, reflect and lead, listen and lead, but above all *lead!*

Questions for Reflection

- How much of your time do you spend shaping and directing and how much maintaining existing patterns of activity?
- What do you need to stop doing?
- Are there others in your church whose gifts of leadership you should be using?
- Are there specific areas where you need to take on leadership? Offer them to God now and ask for his strength and wisdom.

2   Leaders Establish Vision

The Unimaginable Power of Vision

> If you do not know where you are going you are bound to end up somewhere else. (Mark Twain)

Organizations very rarely end up where they want to be unless they are purposeful about it. What is the number one task of the Christian leader? It is to discover what *God* wants for the church or organization he or she leads and then ensure that this is the direction into which all its efforts, activities and resources are focussed.

How? It starts with a vision—a vision before God of what he wants that church to do and be. The vision will be compelling, exciting, challenging and sometimes might feel overwhelming, but if it is from God then the church will have the potential to achieve it. What is the leader's job? It is to receive that vision (directly or indirectly) and express it. It is to step out in faith and lead God's people as they realize and live in all that God has for them. We are people of faith and there is no other place for us to be than in the will of God…for he will 'equip us with everything good for doing his will' (Hebrews 13.21). If it is God's vision you can do it, and if we communicate clearly and pray faithfully together, churches love to grasp vision.

This is how it works with God. Think of some of the great visions of the Bible. Moses led people towards *a land of milk and honey* (Deuteronomy 8.7–10), Jesus left the Great Commission (Matthew 28.18–20). Acts 2 is a compelling vision of 'church.' Revelation provides an enthralling vision of heaven. Each vision, in its unique way, directs, motivates and focuses even thousands of years later in a very different culture.

Do We Not Already Have a Vision?

How would it be if we asked some questions of your church members:

> - Are you excited about being a member of a fantastic team that is transforming your local community, empowered by the Spirit, and bringing people to Christ every week?

- What is your role in God's plan here?

- Why do you come here each week? Custom, tradition, worship, being part of his team?

- How does this church inspire and motivate you in your daily discipleship?

The answers to many of these questions will reflect the presence or absence of God's vision for your church. Many churches are places of indifference, even moaning and criticism. A gospel vision, purposefully followed, transforms our lives and the community around us.

Why Is Vision So Important?

- *It provides focus*—about what we are going to do, and stop doing, the priorities for our money, prayer, time and gifts. Selwyn Hughes describes how we can be 'triflingly employed'—doing things which are intrinsically good but not what God wants us to do. If we are to ensure that the resources available are used to maximize their effectiveness for God's kingdom we need to follow his plan. This is vision.

- *It motivates changed attitudes and behaviours*—if vision requires a change in direction or focus for the church then members need to do things differently. We might stop some meetings to spend more time with non-Christians, or re-order services or buildings, or get up half an hour earlier to pray. The point is that people do not like change—it makes us uncomfortable (try folding your arms backwards to see how that feels). True vision is sufficiently compelling to persuade people to act sacrificially for the joy of building the kingdom.

- *It galvanizes people*—it produces passion and they begin to own it. There is an inner strength to a 'movement,' a campaign, a vision—something that captures hearts and minds. It creates a momentum of its own which helps people to say 'yes,' get involved and be positive about change.

- *It creates accountability*—once a leader has expressed the vision they are accountable for what they believe God wants to do. This helps to reduce drift or softening of purpose. It means that church members should all be able to articulate the vision once it has been communicated, and we will return to this later.

How Do I Receive And Develop Vision?

Let us get to the point here. If you want to develop a clear vision for the church you need to...

1 *Ensure that the church is well taught.* This means exploring the Scriptures so that the development of the vision is clearly framed within biblical principles. It also means that we need to model our practice on men like Nehemiah who took Israel through this process.

2 *Sort out anything which might block your receptiveness to God.* This might mean confronting public sinfulness, dealing with power bases, healing wounded history, or any number of things, but the church needs to be in a place to listen.

3 *Wait on and listen to the Spirit of God.* This is the key, but oddly enough it is the part we find hardest. This waiting will be done individually and with others, and may be focussed around your leadership team if you have one, but must involve...

- teaching the church to listen so that you can do it together.

- waiting with expectancy.

- taking the words that God gives the church seriously.

- looking at what God has placed around you. How do you listen to your community? Why not try mapping local needs? How can you serve your community and love your neighbour?

- visiting, exploring, and reading about things that God is doing elsewhere so that your horizons can be extended, so that your mindset is pushed outside of its usual parameters. Visit the 'worst' to make you sure of what the best may be.

- finding out what your church members think needs to happen. What would they like to see? Is there any consensus? It is a leaders' responsibility to draw the vision together, but *theologically* we need to point out that revelation does not come only to leaders and *practically* it needs to be said that if people are not involved in forming vision then they will not own it and therefore will not take responsibility for it. Involvement leads to ownership. Participation does not mean democracy, but life in a theocracy usually involves a community seeking God's will under wise leadership.

- praying (lots).

4 *Establish the existing resources of the church* — gifts, time, buildings and money. God wants us to use what he has provided — and a great vision will often increase these resources as people respond to it with increased personal commitment.

5 *Come to a decision.* Vision setting is just the start of the adventure and should be the programme for more than a few months of the church's life.

And once the vision has been agreed it needs to be communicated, communicated and communicated some more until everyone gets it and knows what it means for the church and for them.

This means that it needs to be expressed simply and clearly and be aimed at the heart as well as the head. J P Kotter suggests it should take no more than 5 minutes.[1] It should communicate the core of the message and say what really needs to be said. Leadership gurus suggest that vision is usually under-communicated so that people quickly forget what it is about and return to their original behaviour patterns. This communication should be multi-faceted — in your preaching, through vision days, in the way that you lead people into prayer, in key meetings, in finance meetings, one to one, in people's relationships with each other. Above all vision is communicated in what leaders spend their time doing and not doing.

What Do I Do With It Then?

Next we need to develop the plans which will take the church towards its vision. This is one of the areas that churches most frequently baulk at.

'We are a community of believers — our focus is on what we are and what we are becoming. Strategy belongs to the world of business not to God's work.' Strategy does belong to the business world, but only because it works! How much more important is it to build the kingdom well? This is not to take away our identity as sons or daughters but to enhance it, not to remove our dependence on God but to enable it. Strategy is a deliberate expression of radical discipleship.

Jesus was incredibly purposeful and focused during his three years of ministry. He knew what he intended to do and he worked to achieve it. He developed and grew to maturity. He recruited his team, attended to the things he needed to do whilst growing and developing the team to do his work when he had returned to heaven. He targeted the Jews, and left the work with the Gentiles largely to those who came after. He established clear principles for them to follow. Jesus has given us a clear mission — to take the gospel to everyone on this planet. He has also told and shown us how we should live with other members of our church family and in relationship with our local communities, our neighbours. If we are to achieve even some of this we need to be disciples, purposeful and disciplined followers.

Can we say, *'This year our objectives are…And we will achieve them through the following actions…'*? Some call this strategy, some objective setting, some simply what we are trying to get done. Different people will use terms such as aims, objectives, and actions with different interpretations of each. The terminology is not that important. What matters is that there are maybe 8 to 10 major things that the church is planning to achieve in the next year, that contribute to the vision of where the church wants to be and which all have concrete steps to achieving them. Each step or action needs to be:

S pecific

M easurable

A chievable

R ealistic

T ime-limited

And, being realistic, each needs to have a named person taking responsibility for co-ordinating its implementation otherwise the hard bits will be forgotten about.

Example: Vision—To Make the Parish of Snorsley, Downtown a Community Where Everyone Knows Christ

Objective one: To build relationships with those who are not Christians in our community:

	Actions	Co-ordinated By	Completed By	Review
1	Review and reduce the number of church meetings. No-one attends more than one or two meetings per week	Pete	30 July	
2	Teach on importance and place of relationships in evangelism (Sermons / House group study material)	Revd Timms	30 July	
3	50 people to commit to joining a community organization (eg sports club, aerobics class, wine tasting club, PTA)	Ashok	30 Sept	
4	Establish an open social once a month for women in Snorsley	Pauline	31 Jan	
5	Encourage 100 to pray weekly for three of their neighbours	Helen	30 June	

Is There an 'Off-the-Shelf' Vision for Me?

Given that we are all working to the Great Commission, are there any standard objectives that we might see in every church development plan? Well, Jesus' mission statement in Luke 4 expresses that vision in a way that we should all sign up to, but actually this ducks the issue. We are all called to proclaim freedom, release, healing and so on, but the way that we express that locally will be unique. The communities we serve, and each of our churches, their histories, passions and gifts are all very different, and the Spirit works appropriately in each setting. The process of vision-forming is very important. We need to seek out how God wants us to serve him in our local context. There are, however, some common themes that most churches might want to address:

- *Culture* How do we work together as a church? Do we talk together? Is there too little action or too much frenzied activity? Is there too little mutual encouragement or too much self-satisfied pride? Are we reactive or proactive, committed, lazy, optimistic, fearful…? This might be shaped into an objective focussed on the culture we want to see and the actions needed to make it happen.

- *Structures and systems* (ways of working) Do they fit the vision? Is your decision-making rushed, uninformed, ponderous, or do you make decisions quickly and purposefully? Do you need more or fewer committees? Who makes decisions and why? You might have an objective to review structures and systems and then re-align them with effective delivery of the vision.

- *Resources* (gifts, time, prayer and money) Do we have too few, too many? Are they well used? You might need objectives which target the resources needed for your vision.

Questions for Reflection

- Do we have a vision for our church? Is it understood and owned by nearly everyone?

- Do we have a plan shaped by the vision, showing what we want to achieve in the next year, and who is co-ordinating what?

- Is the plan regularly reviewed and does it guide activity?

- Pray through your average week. Do your actions communicate your vision?

3   Leaders Build Teams

Good leaders do not work by themselves.

Jesus did not, neither did most other biblical leaders. Much of the problem for clergy today seems to be that we are trained to work alone and be omni-competent. We do things well, and sometimes better than others in the church could do them now, but because we do not allow others to blossom we rarely see *excellence*. Ministers might be inspiring and able people who can do a lot, but to be *leaders* who grow churches they will need to build a team. How do you go about doing that? The first step is to develop the mindset and practice of delegation.

Delegation—Putting the 'Talents' To Work

Let us be blunt. As you look at your church congregation do you see a field to be ploughed or an army of labourers?

God has provided us or will provide us with everyone we need to do his work, to fulfil his purposes and follow his direction. One of the most important roles of the leader is to see where the Spirit is at work and spot, develop and nurture the gifts, skills and abilities of those in their church. Church leaders are stewards of these resources above all as they seek to fulfil vision.

Leadership Teams
The first and most important step for the church leader is to build a core leadership team. In small churches this may be very small (theory suggests a group of six to eight people in larger churches) but nevertheless we need a team who will help to lead the church. Jesus chose his team for the work he had to do and church leaders need to do likewise. The New Testament guides us on this. We need people who are:

- Gospel-driven
- Spiritually and emotionally mature
- Purposeful
- Humble
- Full of the Holy Spirit

They may have many other qualities (1 Tim 3; Matt 20.25–28), but above all they will be people who enable the team to work positively.

Developing Skills

We must address the problem of the same people doing everything. This starts with *all* members having a good grasp of the vision. Since we are purposeful about developing and using the gifts of every member we go and ask people to do jobs and make absolutely sure that they are fully supported as they do them.

Some members will bring specific skills and experiences to the church. These gifts may be in a fledgling state and people might not even know that they have them, but with careful nurture and training they can have a great impact. How? You need a passion to see the skills and gifts of others developed — and if you have not got one you need to pray like stink for one. Get out amongst the church members, pray for the eyes of the Spirit and look for talent and ability — and do not be afraid to ask people to work!

Prayer

Then we pray for them to be anointed for the task. This can be in public or private, but this is God's work, and prayer and the authority of the Holy Spirit is vital to it. Once you have prayed you continue to pray. As leader of the church you pray regularly and faithfully for everyone who leads under you. How else will they lead?

Training

Throughout our ministry we need to ensure that gifts are developed through good training. Could each worker have a personal development plan — identifying courses, software, books, time-out, mentoring, or visits that would give them opportunity to develop gifts? Is it surprising that children are bored in Sunday School when we jump at anyone who gives the slightest hint of interest in children's work, provide little or no training for them and no supportive supervision? It is not the fault of the volunteer. We must ensure that that we identify real gifts with wisdom and insight, that people know what is expected of them and that they are trained, supported and encouraged in their service. We need to invest money in training and development but there are also many churches and para-church organizations which have skilled secular trainers in their congregations. Why do not we get together and use these people in the church (as we are trying to do in this booklet)?

Supervision

Staff should have regular (monthly) supervision and support. This means meeting with their line manager to discuss how things are going, to problem solve and to plan together. For volunteers this *might* be more informal and less frequent. If we are about God's work then supporting his workers well is really important.

When you look at your church, who is the talent spotter? Who has the gift of discerning people's gifts? (By this we mean those things that they are anointed to do excellently, not just gaps they can fill.) How do you spot gifts, especially in newcomers? Is this done systematically or does your church have a large hole in its gifts' purse? Nothing beats spending time with people doing ordinary things. Is there an expectation that all members will actively participate in the church's life?

Secondly, if you are to build and lead a team you need to be very honest with yourself about your leadership style.

Leadership Style—Collie or Rottweiler?

There has been a lot written about leadership styles. Most of us will have seen very different leadership styles at work or church or socially…from the Rottweiler—'do this do that, and by tomorrow'—whom we dare not even approach, to the lovable spaniel with lots of licks and affection but no results.

Experience suggests that there is no one ideal leadership style, but that we need to adapt to the people we lead and where they are, to the circumstances we face and to our main purposes. This is described in the literature as situational leadership. You will probably have a style which comes most naturally to you and it is right to be who God has made you to be. The vital thing is to be aware of your natural style and use it in the service of Christ. Your style must always be subject to biblical values in leadership. Space prevents a fuller study, but even a cursory glance shows that Christlike leaders will:

- lead people to Christ
- build up not destroy
- serve those they lead
- treat people as human and individual
- believe in people's potential

A comprehensive study of motivation at work developed 12 questions that every employee needs to be able to answer positively if they are to function well at work:

1 Do I know what is expected of me?
2 Do I have the materials and equipment to do my job well?
3 At work do I have the opportunity to do what I do best every day?
4 In the last seven days have I received recognition or praise for what I do well?

5 Does my superior or someone at work seem to care about me as a person?

6 Is there someone at work who encourages my development?

7 Do my opinions seem to count?

8 Is what I am doing making a difference?

9 Are my co-workers committed to doing quality work?

10 Do I have a best friend at work?

11 In the last 12 months have I talked with someone about my progress?

12 This year have I had the opportunity at work to learn and grow?[2]

These are good questions to ask in a church. As David Watson once remarked after an embarrassing introduction, 'even a donkey works better with an occasional pat on the back!' Leaders must protect these needs in whatever style they can. De Pree wraps this up in what he calls participatory management—involving people in the organization so that they feel part of it and committed to it.[3]

Thirdly you need to set about team building.

Team Building

Leaders lead teams because teams are more powerful and effective than individuals. Leaders bring together gifted individuals who work and pray effectively together and present a cohesive and powerful force for change. Purposeful leaders take time to develop their teams as Jesus did. This is a skilled and demanding task.

Great teams consist of people with individual skills and abilities *and* the ability to work well with others—team players. You will be familiar with individuals of great skill who cause unending friction and disruption when put together with others. So in choosing your team there needs to be a combined focus on individual gifting *and* team dynamics.

Bill Hybels, the leader of the largest church in the West, suggests three criteria for selecting team members:[4]

1 **Character**—how is their walk with Jesus? Is there evidence of honesty, teachability, humility, courage, reliability and a willingness to work hard?

2 **Competence**—aim high and go for people who are already making a difference in their work, community or church.

3 **Chemistry**—do I get on with this person and will they fit in and gel with the rest of the team?

Dee Hock, who once managed Visa worldwide, suggests you recruit first on the basis of integrity; second, motivation; third, capacity; fourth, understanding; fifth, knowledge; and last and least, experience. His rationale is that without integrity, motivation is dangerous; without motivation, capacity is impotent; without capacity, understanding is limited; without understanding, knowledge is meaningless; and without knowledge, experience is blind. There is much wisdom here.

Team Roles

Before you recruit you need to know what you want someone to do. What role will they have in fulfilling the vision? A clear job description really helps with that. What is the role of the church warden, the PCC Member, the youth leader? A survey of the British workforce in 2001 found that 85% did not know what their job was really about. They knew what they had to do but had no real idea of the true purpose of their role. No-one had told them. Do you know what you want your paid and volunteer staff to achieve? Do they?

Do you know what you want your paid and volunteer staff to achieve?

Belbin suggests that great teams have team members who embody eight team roles with most of us having one or two dominant team roles. (As examples of the eight: the 'shaper' has drive and a readiness to challenge inertia, the 'completer finisher' follows through and ensures things get finished, the 'plant' provides imagination and creativity.) Teams struggle when one or more of these team roles are missing and/or there is a preponderance of others. The team that generates great ideas probably has at least one 'plant,' but may lack the person skilled at knowing the great ideas from the daft ones (the 'monitor evaluator'). Does your team have both a plant and a monitor evaluator? (Belbin provides a simple questionnaire to help you with this.[5]) Why is there unresolved in-fighting within the team? One reason may be the lack of the 'team-worker' with the skills and heart to spot differences and concerns within the team and a natural aptitude to keep people working together.

Character Types

A second consideration is the character types within a team. Why does John remain so quiet when we know he is really knowledgeable in a certain area? Why do many decisions seem to be badly worked out?

Keirsey helpfully provides a short questionnaire to help analyse your team (see www.keirsey.com). Do you have a well-rounded team able to advance their area of the work? Even when you do, teams made up of the right roles and a balance of character types will sometimes fail to work effectively. Dysfunctional teams often have the following five problems:[6]

1 An *absence of trust* among team members. Essentially, this stems from their unwillingness to be vulnerable within the group. Team members who are not genuinely open with one another about their mistakes and weaknesses make it impossible to build a foundation for trust.

2 This failure to build trust is damaging because it sets the tone for the *fear of conflict*. Teams that lack trust are incapable of engaging in unfiltered and passionate debating of ideas. Instead, they resort to veiled discussions and guarded comments.

3 A lack of healthy conflict is a problem because it leads to a *lack of commitment*. Without having aired their opinions in the course of passionate and open debate, team members rarely, if ever, buy into and commit to decisions, though they may feign agreement during meetings.

4 Because of this lack of real commitment and 'buy-in,' team members develop an *avoidance of accountability*. Without committing to a clear plan of action, even the most focused and driven people hesitate to challenge their peers on actions or behaviour that seem counterproductive.

5 Failure to hold one another accountable creates an environment where the fifth dysfunction can thrive. *Inattention to results* occurs when team members put their individual needs (such as ego, career development or recognition) or even their areas of concern above the collective goals of the team.

And so, like a chain with just one link broken, teamwork deteriorates across the board when dysfunction is allowed to flourish.

On the other hand there are five foundational stones for an effective team. A positive, loving, cohesive team will:

1 Trust each other
2 Embrace conflict and engage in unfiltered debate
3 Commit to decisions and plans of action
4 Hold one another accountable for delivering against those plans
5 Focus on the achievement of collective results

And if you look at the disciples in the gospels and Acts you could tick off these five countless times.

Choosing, developing, and leading great teams is a major and challenging role for the leader—but it is a key part of our service. The most precious 'talents' church leaders have been given are not financial, but the gifts and abilities of all those who serve Christ through their local church. We have the honour of channelling those gifts in line with God's vision for our local church to his greater glory, and 'whoever has will be given more' (Matthew 25.29).

Questions for Reflection

- Does your church nurture and develop fledgling gifts? How might it do so? Who spots them?

- How might you encourage a culture of 'volunteering' or even 'tithing time' in your church?

- What teams exist in your church and how well are they working?

- What new teams are needed and what should the membership look like?

- As a leader how well do I address the needs of those I lead?

- Have you built your leadership team? Who is in it and why? Are there any gaps? How would you know?

4

Leaders are Growth People

The Brilliant Leader—Person Spec and Job Description

Much has been written about what makes a great leader and you will have your own views on what is important. What is in your job description and person specification for a great leader?

Faith

In a Christian context true leaders are always people who walk closely with God. *Christian* leadership can only be that if the leader has a strong and vibrant faith. This means that your key responsibility is your own spiritual growth. All leaders, even you, need to be accountable to others, in just the same (real) way as everyone within a church should be accountable to the leadership. And if you are the senior leader this will probably mean a real relationship with a 'mentor' outside your local context. Do you have that? This walk with God is reflected in the love we have for him and for others... and without love we are nothing at all.

This also means that Christian leaders have to be both called and anointed by God for the task in hand. God calls the most unlikely people (Gideon springs to mind), but when he anoints them they are able. And if God does not build the house, then the labour is in vain.

Vision
Leaders will be visionary and we have already discussed this. They may not be the people who come up with the key ideas but they will have the ability to pull the vision together, and this will energize and enthuse them. If you are not excited, stretched, and challenged by a vision, who else is going to be?

Purpose
Leaders will be purposeful, able to plan and follow through. They turn vision into clear processes of action and work with others to see its fulfilment. They will not be ashamed of success or growth.

Courage

God says 'Do not be afraid' 366 times in the Bible

Leaders cannot be faint-hearted; great leaders have a major helping of courage. Setting vision and direction clearly and purposefully will mean some things are not going to happen. Someone will be bound to be hurt by this. We have feelings too and it is not easy to cope with confrontation or brown-enveloped letters of complaint. That is one reason why a supportive leadership team is very important. Leadership takes great courage. God's words to Joshua are repeated several times: 'Be strong and courageous...Be strong and very courageous...Be courageous and courageous.' (Joshua 1.6–7). God says 'Do not be afraid' 366 times in the Bible—that is one for every day of the year, even in a leap year. 'For God did not give us a spirit of timidity, but a spirit of power, of love and of self-discipline' (2 Timothy 1.7). So let us fan our gifts from him into flame and let us start praying for the gift of boldness.

People Skills
John Kotter suggests that for significant change to work, it requires the commitment of *all* senior managers, and 75% of all first line managers. In a church this means that it is essential for the leadership team and important for the decision-making body (church council, church membership) to be together if change is to be effective. This can be hard as in a time of change 20–25% of those involved will follow the vision, a similar number will be strongly opposed, and the reminder will usually be undecided.

So your inter-personal skills are really important. Do you listen and hear your people? Do you give them time? Are you warm, appreciative and encouraging? If we take God's investment in our ministry seriously then we will recognize that the Spirit will convict people, his vision will inspire them, but for many he will use your inter-personal skills to move them out of the 50% into the committed, and from being opposed to merely questioning.

Communication Skills
Your communication skills are also vital. Why are we so wedded to pulpits and lecterns, barriers between us and our listeners? Nearly all modern communication skills courses encourage us to connect by getting close. Why not video members of the preaching team and give and receive constructive feedback on what is done well and what could be improved?

Our most effective form of communication is our actions. This is likely to be the main way which your church members evaluate you. It is no use saying, 'We welcome you to our church today' and then explaining nothing of the service to newcomers, disappearing after worship rather than chatting over coffee, having spent the time before the service huddled in the vestry rather than smiling on the door. As they say in the prison chapel here, who cares if you can talk the talk if you do not walk the walk?

Humility
Finally, leaders need massive dollops of humility. If you are to be a great leader then you will have to rely on the Giver not the gift or the gifted, on the Lord himself. Effective Christian leadership recognizes that our ability to lead comes from God, is empowered by him through his Holy Spirit and without him is but a resounding gong or a clanging cymbal.

Energizing Teams and their Members

So, you have set your vision and communicated it directly and clearly. You have planned how to deliver it and built teams to work it out…what next? Well actually, even when these things are coming together we need to ensure that people remain motivated and committed. Church leaders lead volunteers. This is their primary resource and let us recognize that most are unpaid and have their own ideas of what a church 'should' do and are therefore potentially difficult to lead.

Leaders will have an ingrained philosophy or belief of how people are motivated and what makes them tick. What do you believe energizes people?

Kotter emphasizes the power of vision expressed through the actions of the leader in galvanizing and motivating workers, firing up the enthusiastic, convincing the unconvinced, and drawing the uncommitted out of their comfort zone into new ways of doing and being.

Charles Handy describes a psychological contract between the employee/volunteer and the employer. He suggests that employees' contracts are made up of two elements: the pay and conditions; and the values and purpose of the organization.[7] Workers are prepared to be paid less if the vision, values and mission of the organization are closely aligned with their own. Volunteers have no financial benefit so the correlation of their values with the organization's is fundamental. If they see the two separating then they will become de-motivated or leave. If they feel they are very closely aligned then they will work hard and be fully committed. Consider the commitment of the Greenpeace volunteer—or the disillusionment caused by escalating salaries of senior staff in voluntary organizations. Removing the pews, changing the liturgy or using fewer hymns may not seem significant in the wider vision but they can represent 'marks' of a changed vision to those who hold them dear. Handy might argue that the church member may see such changes as breaking the psychological contract between the church member and the church. He would not be surprised at how impassioned consideration of such changes can become. For him developing vision is about renegotiating a contract or bringing clarity to what the vision and values really are.

Hertzberg carried out some fundamental research into what people found the greatest motivators at work.[8] This was originally done in the late 50s and early 60s and has been re-worked many times with its original findings confirmed. The top four motivators were:

Achievement—people are motivated by being purposeful and delivering. They do not naturally slack. In the right context we enjoy working hard to make things happen. The epistles exhort us to 'run the race.' Jesus was not afraid to ask people to work hard, and his work allows people to achieve. Can we say the same?

Recognition—having achieved, people like to be praised, encouraged and recognized for what they do. This is not about pride but being rightly pleased and satisfied with what they have done. We Brits struggle to give praise, but all research suggests it is really important to people. How many people have you praised or recognized in the last week—and how many people have praised you? Do we have to wait till the end to hear 'well done good and faithful servant'?

Responsibility—people thrive on a challenge and being given responsibility. They do not see this as onerous, providing it is within a supportive organizational culture, but relish a degree of autonomy with which to make a difference. How skilled are you at delegating...really?

The Nature of the Work itself—is the work interesting? Does it have purpose? Is it intrinsically beneficial? How well do we communicate the vital nature of tasks that need doing? Do we ask someone to make tea, or be part of a team developing hospitality?

Paul highlights Barnabas's skills as an encourager, and the apostles renamed him to reflect this primary skill. Churches can be difficult places to be part of, particularly if they are going through a time of change and facing the challenges that Satan throws in our path. But leadership should always encourage and nurture, build up and equip—not least because inevitably such leaders are themselves encouraged and supported by the teams they have built. This 'grace-cycle' (the opposite to a vicious circle) is vital to a life of ministry.

Running the Race—Developing and Sustaining Great Leaders

Research into effective leadership shows that longevity in a leadership role, particularly ten years plus, has the greatest lasting impact. It suggests that it takes an absolute minimum of four years for cultural change to take root and usually six to eight years for real change to happen. Leadership and lasting change require stickability and a sustained ministry. So what can leaders do to sustain themselves long term?

Stephen Covey provides some helpful steps:

1 **Be proactive**—you may not be able to decide what challenges or difficulties meet you head on, but you can decide how you will respond to them. Look ahead and act accordingly rather than waiting to be hit by the next problem or crisis. Know what you can influence or change and what you must leave untouched.

2 **Begin with the end in mind**—know where you are heading, your priorities and stick to them. 'Let us fix our eyes on Jesus, the author and perfecter of our faith, who for the joy set before him, endured the cross, scorning its shame and sat down at the right hand of the throne of God' (Hebrews 12.2).

3 **Put first things first**—what are the eight or ten most important things for you to do? Good leaders manage their time well and know how to say 'no.' They are also flexible. If you put your weekly activities (both planned and unplanned) into the diagram on the right which boxes would they fill?

1 Urgent Important	2 Not Urgent Important
4 Urgent Unimportant	3 Not Urgent Unimportant

> Covey suggests that we spend far too little time in quadrant 2 and far too much time in the last two. Try noting activities you plan to do or have done through the week in these four boxes. Are you putting first things first? What can you cut to insert some balance?

All leaders need to be developed. Warren Bennis is very clear that leaders are made not born. Scripture is clear that leaders are chosen and anointed by God.[9] So there is hope for all of us(!) but we do need to spend time developing and training leaders including ourselves. What does a great leadership programme look like? It is interesting that most conferences in the UK on Christian leadership are not about leadership skills but about the ministry of the church—effective cells, great preaching, prayer ministry. These are all really important but they are not leadership skills.

Leadership development is a quadrant 2 activity and many leaders will suggest that they are too busy to fit in any training or development. The implication of not attending to your development (and others') will be that you will become less effective over time. Every marathon runner trains.

Training will be different for different people. For some it will be leadership training courses and conferences, for some, if not all, mentoring from a skilled leader and mentor. We need to spend time with others, take time out to think, ponder, study Scripture and pray, and visit and watch successful leadership elsewhere. For all of us, though, it will mean quality time spent with the Lord. The godly nature of our calling reinforces rather than removes our need for development. We need to invest in our leaders and especially in ourselves, for godly leaders are never ashamed of growth.

Leaders need to have balance in their lives. We cannot live all our time as leaders and do it well. We need time for our families and friends, for relaxing, for study and many other things. However impossible this seems with the pressures on your time at the moment, it is vital.

Questions for Reflection

- How do you motivate those around you? Do you need a new strategy for this?
- Who motivates and encourages you?
- Have you encouraged each person you work with this week?
- How balanced and sustainable is your lifestyle?
- What growing do you need to do in the next six months and how are you going to do it?

5 Leaders Go For It!

Finally we need to stress that leaders lead!

They do it, they go for it, they jump in, they take risks, they make mistakes, they press on, they get on with it, and they are the ones that achieve. Churches can be tough beasts to lead, but that is our calling so let us get on with it.

Tackling Church Culture

Culture is the way that people work together in an organization, the unseen but immensely strong forces or values that determine how things are done. Culture can be a force for good, holding things together, creating the intangible *esprit de corps* that bonds and unites. It can also be a strong force resisting change, dragging people back from doing what needs to be done. It has been described positively as the glue that holds everything together and negatively as glue on your feet which stops you moving forward.

Culture can be the glue that holds everything together or the glue on your feet which stops you moving forward

Some examples of elements of church culture are:

- *Celebratory*—positive and thankful, celebrating great things that God has done.

- *Reactive*—rarely looking forward or proactively establishing what it is going to do. 'What do we do now that there are only three children involved in Sunday School?'

- *Hierarchical*—all authority is held 'at the top' and few people feel able to make decisions even about very minor matters. Decisions need to be referred to the Vicar or Mrs Crinkley-Bottom who does the flowers!

- *Openness*—there is a free flow of views and perspectives and people are able to express their opinions and know they are heard even when they are in marked contrast to the views of others.

- *Traditional*—'the King James was good enough for Jesus and Saul of Tarsus and it is good enough for me!'

The Bible provides us with significant hints towards what church culture should be like through what our values should be. One cannot easily imagine a church where people are not encouraged to be open (to God and each other), or where thankfulness or mutual encouragement and appreciation are not important. However, we often do not consider explicitly what our culture or values are, or what we want them to be. Most organizations, when trying to change or develop to maximize their effectiveness, will name the culture they want to achieve and will focus on actions to achieve it.

In exploring existing culture we need to ask three questions:

What are the artefacts of our church? These are our visible organizational structures and processes, like our language (Authorized, NIV or The Message), our use of technology (flannel boards or data projectors), or our structures (PCC meeting or chat with church leader). All provide clues about the culture of the organization.

What are our espoused values? These are the stated values of an organization. They predict well enough what people should/ought to say in a variety of situations but may be out of line with what they will actually do in situations where those values should in fact be operating.

What are our basic assumptions? These are what we really believe at a deeper level (usually so deep that we act without questioning these assumptions). Because we neither confront nor debate them they are very difficult to change. Change can only occur if we re-examine and challenge some of the most stable aspects of our internal belief systems. This causes high levels of anxiety. Cultural change is about this development of basic assumptions and is difficult and time–consuming. It is, however, vital for the leader to address these foundational beliefs and to support people through the anxious unsettled period that accompanies any change. One of the main reasons why people are so turned off by church is that they perceive a huge gap between our espoused (biblical) values and our basic assumptions (reflected in how we live day by day). We say we welcome everyone, but so frequently 'our touch does not match our words.'

> *We say we welcome everyone, but so frequently 'our touch does not match our words'*

For example, someone might say of their church, 'Our existing culture is bureaucratic with power and control residing firmly at the centre. Endless committees meet to make few decisions, and simply pass on recommendations to a central decision-making body.'

Desired Culture: Empowered Disciples Working in Common Direction

Actions:

1 Establish which decisions need to be made centrally and which can be made locally.
2 Agree the objectives/remit of the decentralized groups.
3 Be clear about what values they should work to.
4 Commission the group(s) in a main service, asking for the power of the Spirit to rest upon them for this task.
5 Support them; back them up even when they make mistakes.
6 Supervise them, urging them on or restraining them if it is necessary.
7 Trust them and God to do what is before them…keep praying and keep letting go!

Charles Handy has suggested four cultures that describe most organizations. Most prevalent in churches are what he calls the Zeus culture and the Apollo culture. The Zeus culture is described as a spider's web with the centre, the spider, being the leader. The relationship to the spider matters more than any formal title or position. Power and influence are determined by how close you are to Zeus. With Apollo the organization is rational with lots of order and rules. People and committees have roles and purposes.

In churches we often see Zeuses, powerful leaders who have shaped every aspect of the church. They decide what is sung in worship, the colour of the carpet in church, what the maintenance budget is spent on, and who does what. The strength of this culture is rapid decision-making, with clear focus. Its weaknesses are that the quality and scope of decision-making depends on the calibre of Zeus, and that members are dis-empowered.

The Apollo culture is excellent in times of stability, when tomorrow is likely to look like the day before, because it works on stability and predictability. Its weakness is that it cannot respond to changing environments easily or quickly because it works on complicated systems and procedures.

Given the challenges we face in churches, surely we need something of a blend between several cultures; we need rapid centralized decision-making over major decisions and direction. We need freedom for smaller teams to work with specific briefs, building strong community in an age of fragmentation. We need to work within the overall values and be free to create, and it is worth investing time formulating and expressing these values as clearly as you do your vision.

This leadership business is dynamite. Every major event in the Bible and in church history is led by someone whom God has raised up for the task. It is never possible to see beforehand what will happen and the most extraordinary results spring from the most unlikely of sources, so will you let God bless the world through you?

It Is No Rehearsal—Go For It!

After analysing organizations which brought about significant change, David Schwartz came to one key conclusion:

> Leadership is everything. Organizations which bring about significant and sustained change have one thing in common—unusually gifted and able leaders.[10]

Leadership may not be *everything* but God has made you a steward of the collective gifts of his people, and of their potential to change the world. As a leader your task is hugely demanding and you need to continue to build your leadership skills—but even more than that, you need to use them.

Max De Pree states:

> When we think about leaders and the variety of gifts people bring to corporations and institutions, we see that the art of leadership lies in polishing and liberating and enabling those gifts...In short the true leader enables his or her followers to realize their full potential.[11]

As Christian leaders we lead on our knees so that God may be glorified in all we do and that our legacy will be a church growing in Christ.

If you are a church leader then grow in your gifting, delight in releasing others into theirs, and lead the church. That is why the Lord has put you here and you have only got one life to do it in!

Questions for Reflection

- What is your existing culture? Simply asking what is working and what is not working and why will generate lots of information about the strengths and weaknesses of existing culture.

- Consider what elements of culture you would want to keep, which ones you would want to drop and which ones you would like to develop. How can you do this in the next 12 months?

- What are the values of your church?

- How will you grow as a leader of God's church over the next 12 months?

Useful Reading

J Adair, *Effective Strategic Leadership* (London: Macmillan, 2002)

R M Belbin, *Management Teams—Why They Succeed or Fail* (Oxford: Butterworth-Heinemann Ltd, 1981)

W Bennis, *On Becoming a Leader* (London: Arrow Books Limited, 1998)

S Covey, *The Seven Habits of Highly Effective People* (London: Simon and Schuster, 1989)

P F Drucker, *The Essential Drucker* (Oxford: Butterworth-Heinemann, 2001)

J P Kotter, *Leading Change* (Boston: Harvard Business School Press, 1996)

M De Pree, *Leadership is an Art* (New York: Doubleday Publishing, 1989)

L Gerstner, *Who Says Elephants Can't Dance* (New York: Harper Collins Publishers Inc, 2002)

R Greenleaf, *Servant Leadership* (New York: Paulist Press, 1977)

C Handy *The Gods of Management* (Reading: Arrow Books Ltd, 1995)

B Hybels, *Courageous Leadership* (Grand Rapids: Zondervan, 2002)

S Johnson, *Who Moved My Cheese* (London: Vermillion, 1998)

M Pedler, J Burgoyne, T Boydell, *The Learning Company* (Maidenhead, McGraw-Hill Book Company Europe, 1991)

E Schein, *Organizational Culture and Leadership* (San Francisco: Jossey-Bass, 1992)

R Warren, *The Purpose Driven Church* (Grand Rapids: Zondervan, 1995)

W C Wright, *Relational Leadership* (Carlisle: Paternoster, 2000)

Notes

1   J P Kotter, *Leading Change* (Boston: Harvard Business School Press, 1996) p 72.

2   M Buckingham and C Coffman, *First Break All The Rules—What the World's Greatest Managers Do Differently* (Simon and Schuster, 1999).

3   M DePree, *Leadership is an Art* (New York: Doubleday Publishing, 1989).

4   B Hybels, *Courageous Leadership* (Grand Rapids: Michigan, Zonderman, 2002) pp 73–82.

5   R M Belbin, *Management Teams—Why They Succeed or Fail* (Oxford: Butterworth-Heinemann Ltd, 1981).

6   *The Five Dysfunctions of a Team: A Leadership Fable* by Patrick M Lencioni, April 2002.

7   C Handy, *Understanding Organizations* (London: Penguin, 1993) pp 47–49.

8   F Herzberg, 'One more time: How do you motivate employees?' in R M Steers and L W Porter (eds), *Motivation and Work Behaviour* (New York: McGraw-Hill, 1975) pp 91–194.

9   I am thinking of Romans 12.8, but it is also clear that God anoints leaders with his Spirit in the Old Testament, and interesting that an apostle is chosen in Acts 1 to carry on the leadership role.

10 D Schwartz, *Crossing the River* (Brookline Press, 1992) p 217.

11 M DePree, *Leadership is an Art* (New York: Doubleday Publishing, 1989) p 10.